Glengarry

rob mclennan

TALONBOOKS

Talonbooks
PO 2076, Vancouver, British Columbia, Canada V6B 3S3
www.talonbooks.com

Typeset in Adobe Garamond Pro.
Printed and bound in Canada on 100% post-consumer recycled paper.

First Printing: 2011

The publisher gratefully acknowledges the financial support of the Canada Council for
the Arts; the Government of Canada through the Book Publishing Industry Development
Program; and the Province of British Columbia through the British Columbia Arts
Council and the Book Publishing Tax Credit for our publishing activities.

rob mclennan regularly posts reviews, essays, interviews and
other notices at robmclennan.blogspot.com.

LIBRARY AND ARCHIVES CANADA CATALOGUING IN PUBLICATION

McLennan, Rob, 1970–
    Glengarry / Rob McLennan.

Poems.
ISBN 978-0-88922-662-3

    I. Title.

PS8575.L4586G55 2011   C811'.54   C2010-907128-X

What has come to interest me right now is what I suppose you can call the dream of origins.

Robert Kroetsch, *The Long Poem Anthology*

Contents

glengarry: open field

(a postscripted journal)

Preconceptions of landscape differ from their surroundings.
Lise Downe, *Disturbances of Progress*

– making landscape of self,
the stopped line or silence, –
Barry McKinnon, *Pulp/Log*

(the task: to make visible   the farm, the heart, the centre
Barry McKinnon, *The Centre*

In the minds of many Canadians, the word Glengarry evokes
a great feeling of nostalgia.
Canadian Forum (1942)

*

then, for instance, this manner of discursive
                                field; a lawnmower big as cars,
build consequence of struggle, belonging
& cultural verve

                        is this language
or negation; the Angus Grey rebuilt,
teen arson; all that frustration
                                on highland grounds
        when graduation, he could have
              simply left

                        ; what can't redo, go back

                        a means
of plenty; Holsteins roam slow fields
; the authorial function of deer
        of wolf or moose as wanderers, a thoroughfare,

                        as the fox keeps close to ground
                        ; in the process of writing, itself

*

says little, nothing; *am writing this*
                    so rob mclennan will understand
            , in pooling rough along fence lines
& posts, an apparatus of familiarity

                                moves, but does not
, further claims of open field, open score
would stars keep distant still, in love
        w/ experience

pointing produces, gestures; Copernicus,
        & the summer plot; this land
knows seasons, sun, wind & snow; sleep
                        in parallel wonder

                        , near Biblical

*

North West Company charm; speak as almost
nothing else; the same
                dozens of tellings but little
variety, else; a distraction of beer,
golden burst,

                    far-flung immediate,
drained by excess; stone cairn,
dissolute & broken; plaid heart
                strong & stoic tweed, incised

*

how to be, the long grass slide
        behind barn, smoking cigarettes
empty silo a skeletal, wake
a dead thing; where the wind

                never hardens, mud
; chronicle of forest, axe; soldiers
to barons to farmers; Williamstown,
Williamsburg, New Johnstown (Cornwall)

                        , where Sir John
Johnston organized,
a barrier; sweeping stones & then stones
                open boat, a drift

feed breaking waters,
                        Caledonia Springs
        & hotel, royalty in waves
a hundred more back years

without a trace, a trace

*

father his father & his; my sister,
                                        partner, children; these
roots beyond; field poetics sky blue
                            paint in cloud
        & a hummingbird, squirrels

                    if implement a scenery, sun
inherited structure; shadings, lyric
movement, are there trees
                            beyond in clear

                                    imperfect swallows
intersect sun & moon; three days of cars
kick gravel up & dust,
                                    can hear
                    before horizon

*

exhibition of space in white straw hat,
a natural history
                        of Eastern Ontario,
            network of claims & ancient memory, St.
Raphael's Church & the Battle of Chrysler's Farm,
                        dynamic, transmittable

                        Simon Fraser buried in
& over; land returned, constitution
of old forms changed & reconfigured;
            the skull beneath sun, is
                        the skull in the field

            , a dead cow
                        , the stone barn

*

snap over branch, begin; former neighbour
          who spread her father's ash
in the creek behind acres, well after
          they'd moved; maple scent

through boiling spring house set off
smoke detectors; mound
          of damp earth a ruin once
sugar shack my grandfather built
decades gone;

          one hundred more feet from
apple trees where schoolhouse hands held
; where his father learned
          the strap & what else; how to read,
perhaps

          the earth remembers every scratch
& scar & step, if you know
          where to look,

                    the way of assembling

*

the sky rolls field; of copper, soybean, corn
                    , pyramid straw hay
& field mice; holes poke siding
                            pellets pigeons missed
, blue sky mustard, uncoil over

                            you want to love, but still
release no sounds; a stubborn violent
heritage; constant
        maintenance,
                            doorknob
falls, a cow through fence
& neighbour calls
                        , smoke
            horizons, any eye
can pinpoint farm, ten miles; building,

*

in the natural earth rise to trees, oversize
                    backdrop blue & billboard, spotlight
livestock & next highway line
                            , to differentiate ourselves
        from the past; a fury, richness

                    animated from Gaelic
& old Bibles, twin lines at odds
        technique
                            , & dangerous in their
                implications

                            seeking a series of abbreviations,
behind the motion of naming, the bar opens
        w/ another; once the general store
                , then a candy for kids, the owner old
                                        & widowed

set back, watching television; what town kids
                            could grab

        before she caught them; three at a time,

*

if death speaks; pluralism

     John Deere, Ford
, a texture, close to world tents
    , quilt; homemade applesauce

sky suspends both ends
of possibility; green lines, highway
      strafing north & south,
   roaring east & farther west,
    & undersmell
       of pulp mill
        , international bridge

a construction of houses in the village
      , conscious of common
   function; creating meaning from fields, thin
       & continually pushed

& town not yet; village-thick, pulsing
   object growth

*

a mystery of boxes; the main thrust here
   is age; telephone party lines
& Vachon bread man Wednesdays,
Steve the hired man who lived in '70s room

      no longer spare, once a sister
; Eastern breeder an ashtray & instant coffee
brought out from hiding; once
   twice a year
       is this memory
or romanticism, a clear view of fate
& lost world; ways of listening
    & speaking
       no longer

he would know the names of trees
& leaves & cows, but rarely birthdays

*

how away is away, circling claims
      as opening; prolonging
opening field;
                all paths to Sunday,
morning serene then singing,
         family pews, minister extolling
out from the silence, silent
                    , choir robes
from grandparent days
in musty church,
            torches
    through bush-league miles & religious revivals
from 1860s; talk

          as yesterday;
remember horse-drawn
      only weekly break from work

             , this social

*

would erode strict days, linear leanings
                              w/ snow shovel, lift
              where pile once, two
                       storeys; smoke lift clear
from chimney & rode low ground

                              we in our snowsuits, pounding

hope or dream of escape, this
                   was all this; recorded forever
              in either direction & won

                              obdurate nothing
; where rain hit the field & sang

*

half-open story of what no longer,
          tale told in parting breaths
      & stagnant waters; the body's pale veil,
                    to trick
              us into thinking

if consternation is a way to sink

          of staunch conservatism,
Ontario Protestantism; hard work is the answer
      the failure
        of reward for hard work

              Calvinist patterns
      that repeat, & loop; am dogged,
        doggedness
                herding lines
& memories taste
        in widening arc

      if we know anything; roughneck speech
              rehearsed in shaking light,
        & family unit

*

history written by everything
        history forgets; a chair a charm, held
            & remembered, misremembered, still

    is raining harder now

to pull through the body; find a map of twenty years
& go there; twenty fifty hundred

        swallowed notes
, of road signs never needed, for
      the newness crop
                  , Howard Morrow
Johnny Billinghurst Cameron MacGregor Bill DeHass
      our particular corner   all dead

      thought that they might live forever

       , land I still consider theirs
driving past

if there is no mystery, nothing left to wake

*

if then, reading; stand-in for the past,
                 & spoken; what else
you refuse
                      , repeat the course
of arrival, listless; everything in here
                            repeated,

                              a schoolbook
                              contained

; story exists, am living
the language of it

                    Monkland diner where once spent
                         Christmas Eve,
                                like any diner
          on television; if you'd none to listen,

*

of secrets & toothfairies; rebuild
      of its own foundation, one day lay
my father's bones & his

                 , in this house where we
return; the story of Glengarry
is the story
                  of eternal prodigal, one
can never stray
for long

            intrigue
& bare, nine months, nineteen years,
the roots
           , curse of the passenger ships,
that carried
                   , the *Neptune*

*

necktie dream; Ralph Connor richness
in a dream of sentiment,
the hard-boiled Scot an island
, w/out pretence,
large & echoing; violence, to a man

; Big Rory, the lost hammer swing

ending both a young girl
& his throwing days; faint turquoise slide
St. Lawrence, the borders of Irish
& French; does a hand recall,

stared at by deer
& settlement, burnished tongue the edge
of limb
Lord Simcoe, wet sand
; a resolve marked by passion

the mouth of new world open
, trace the taste of old

: *forgive them*

*

turning in, tepid tongues, passionate rejoinders, anguish
of being, incorporated into
        these knives & rocks
        these fencelines burning
               , path of the world
                    on the page

, can mark a hamlet,
            a hundred
        churchbell years

               translating
a field of vision; when meanings
            mirrored the need
for discomfort, rejection, religion

           , a narrative long fixed

*

called history & pervasive trail
        , off in the woods

Lochiel bait; bare stretch of run
& miracle yawn
                        , grain stick
& provincial blue plaque, hills
relive, revive

                    , words words less words than speaking
written down, unless
        politic or the preacher man, speaking out
for something
                        , choir

if cedars spring & wild berries
        , eat what you can, what
you can't, you can
                        a jar, at least

a dusting ,
years on cellar shelf;

*

there is always the fear
                    of looking back so hard a stare, speak
darkened array
                                white gravestones smooth
, slip names; a nest of collusion,
my mother's car driving
                                    drawn, & endless
        for groceries, the Cornwall superstore

                    remembered & known, for where
we planted; son of son of, daughter
& what history lines that draw
        any, exclude

where days & songs heap upon story,
& make fertile, a hothouse
                    of green image

        & the Raisin River

*

would hold out for sound, suspending flights
               down highway, dirt roads
        a slave to speech; if need
                      a new limit
; what have neither abandoned
                           , left, all points
          to contrary

                , she says
he too: this leaving, left

                    in Heaven ruled by law
                       of wordless voice

               , a series of orders,
        a limit
                  of formal achievement

*

if this goes w/out saying,
                          a perpetual ideal, or
                                    habit
; we would know the world by how it sparkles
        , burns, it smokes;
                a low-ball keening,
the baler through twine,

                        combine hedgerows
        around; familiar utterance
& a silence, unnamed
                        , unmoved

how many times repeated: silence,
        a treble clef of short forks
                        & a likely, beaten path

*

where story in its way begets,
       & speaking some;
    old swimming hole or track in the field,
        or stone we sat on,
                property line,

           , old soccer displays

not a body but being; rocks from field
       to front-end loader,
unbent plow; rise w/ morning & corn; breaks questions
           from answers, no
    holiday or even; opposing touch

, which is negative; whether breaking the conceit, or
       well dry of consequence, garter snakes, behind
              the barn
      , a question of desire,

*

the yard w/ corpse cars & *Hail Marys*
                            , French county corners
            ; a blistering cloud
& ripples, a roster of material
                  in pine

                            , refreshing, am satisfied
a bleakness of biography, what goes on seems ordinary,
endless
          , a drink w/ my sister & Corey
                        in their backyard

& the firepit behind where our grandma
kept compost; her secrets to grave

*

in that hollow that forms on knowing
                              ; wild honey, rebuilding, sweep
the kitchen; the shed he kept nothing so he built
anew

spare parts always kept

                  , let me do the work I need,
try speaking; write down
piano wire, Bible from 1888
                              that hasn't named anyone

since 1950s; in order of introduction,
proximity
                  , not birth

*

palpable, September song; bleating
       harvest & the school bus
top of laneway; one
              & another

      , where we minister

red light to green, open water
, Ontario to Ontario, from
      Lancaster docks
           , new
      & unaligned

a diminishing gesture is made, how ceaseless
is critically barren

    ; we all imagined boundaries

    , theologies built on stony silence

*

Maxville, Moose Creek, Dominionville, Athol, Dunvegan
; Alexandria, Greenfield, Monroe's Mills, Glen
Norman, Summerstown
; weeks in the field; Apple Hill, Tayside, St. Andrew's West, St.

Raphael's, Lancaster, Macdonald's Grove Road

; St. Elmo, Green Valley, Glen Robertson, Glen Nevis, Cornwall, St.
Regis, Williamstown, Monkland, Curry Hill, Pine
Hill, Martintown, Raisin River, South
Nation River, Dyer Road, Sandringham, Laggan, Fassifern, Kirkhill

; Dalhousie Mills, Bainsville, St. Isidore de Prescott,
Avonmore, Loch Garry, Breadalbane, Cashions Glen, Grants
Corners, Glen Walter, Caledonia
Springs

*

prehistory, then, say white folk; Celts
                              , don't remember *any*,
before they; sense of salt
& body's worth; substantial roughness, voyeur

                      , but to fall back

can't step into same water flows,
down w/ gravity, wild grapes on the Raisin River
          sink, then swim; Don's cabin,
Alexandria autumn, when the leaves
                      & high school; Clare's Aunt Tess,

& Uncle Ray;
                          , owed him a pie

      (strawberry rhubarb)

*

a perfectly reasonable ruin, communal gait
in the iron-wrought fence; where old stones
              tumble free; St. Raphael's will,
& Bryan McDonell, last of the last

                 1984: mother arrived to say her mother-in-law,
Alexandria dawn, Labour Day noon
the only time I remember her going in
     to hospital; grandmother

                    the one they say
you never leave; hospital blue
like Hotel California; The Eagles
where Ann-Marie,
      ex-wife, was born

               like an ode
     to its properties

*

all of which we don't, about; still
                        waiting for mine, my twentysomething
daughter; nails, nose piercing, shape
        loud music literate; bruised qualms

                don't listen to anything; one removed

don't be literal; a bit of breeze, palms
        brushed on slacks from the dust
                        under speech, small
motions fall; the workshirt he wears
                from Co-op, St. Isidore

                , that is, if I remember
            ; the architect of stony haunches, &
                            long afternoons

*

don't remember anything about purpose,
                                        virgin trail
                in forests; walking
                        from St. Lawrence;
to the point of solving difficulties formal,
the passage of technique

                                                defeat
or success, I don't yet know; between the mind
of modern body & the land, if
        there is even
                        lake & the cairn

writing best; needless to say,
        & flowers, adapted from the beach
                                        , uncertain shore

; a river is always certain

*

a hole to be filled & a hole, followed the course
              of *any* river; the Grand (Ottawa)
        where logs went, hewn
                  & hustled,

                          Company men
                & Champlain, displaced by chaos,

    the only doctor his cold Maxville hands

              Laggan, meaning *low-lying ground*
the same Gaelic as *Logan* (root), where
              basin or fall
       , collects; blackened changes
             to posthumous remains

nothing dies in spring; heifers bleating born
         out of winter's difficulties

*

in regards to the cut; as if it were conclusion
                    the pioneer stage of roads
through shallows; to fill w/ stones

        tales of the Canada Atlantic; cart before horse

houses in course, cornerstone
                    of ambitious capital;
            swamp

                                    if the practice is pleased
& temperature fading

                driving three years of county, dry

; *a beer in hand is worth*

*

the thought of a good argument, &
unfinished bay
                              , might have missed the mills
        or cheese factory; staunch Tory
by days, amid preparations

                              for real work
; rake drawn by teams
, to furrow rows, the horse slid
              & the forks; no matter how far,
        a feeling of ease

*

         ; the geography
of an imaginary silence, roots in a field & the poetry
       of answering; dumbness

heartwood; generation of hard earth
, landscapes living Loyalist barns
& thick wood cleared

                 characteristic
of the entire nervous system; generative,
1812 scars, the stone-green, logs hewn
         to float Ottawa barges,
the immaculate separation of Long Sault,
Calvinist ideal, dour Protestantism,

      singing *holy holy holy*

    if they spoke at all; read
         clear on rock face,

*

suspended a still surface, the northern lights
       sprinkle across dirt road,
endless bush, too thick to walk
less tractor trail

               a John Deere wilderness
of dairy & obsessive behaviour; a tactile
whisper of every old
       unspoken Scot

never enough to not say; profound music
surrounds Loch Garry, wash
       a quarry; what rarely drives
for work; what once a four day walk
from Montreal; two hundred miles

           & never left,

*

how much of the problem
                    is simply to live; Glengarry
grown older, we remain; the history
& the public combined
                            drowned, guffaws
of nineteenth-century flame; do you remember?

    Maxville fire or the bank heist,

                    if you love the stone
or love the tree; remains the same song
hauling hay & hybrid grain corn
                            more than average,
more than letter or light
                            for the next fifteen years

        ; United Counties

*

this is drawn upon townships
                    , traced & retraced
two centuries or more; Old Mill Road,
or on first looking down
                              from Cashions Glen bridge,
an old window, & Bill
MacGillivray's cap
                    , the weeds

            no mistake
                              , grown close to soil,
in neighbouring claims; a boundary lot
& century farm; two cars
        & satellite dish; the cable tower
                    west of village
                              where once sat
        the Ralph Connor schoolhouse

                    now at Upper Canada Village

; if you know where the history, happened

*

a theoretical grid
        of old miles & roads; to wit
, zigzags compensate
     for surveying errors, or difficult terrain
                ; my grandfather

had multiple lives: as farmer, maple-syrup maker,
     Eastern Breeder
                     , completed
         well before I arrived

*

before beginning; a recovering cup
                    of smart models; Long Sault Rapids,
Cornwall Island, "Indian Lands," county
        larger than its boundaries, prescriptive

                        we all know, what

doctors borders & move faith like mountains,
up the south lumbering side, counting logs
        & logs; the Lochinvar Bridge
or hot spot

                    , floating moon

                    , of river
            do know or know

        ; in time would notice

*

Sandringham days, one-room schoolhouse
        & annual social; where maiden grandmother
taught; the *Ontario Reader*, c. 1934
                & the riddle of man
                                        & woman

mauled by gaze of tranquility, light
, stars out in force
                                radio tower's red red blink
        , pollution glow; am witnessing
faith; each day a day
                that will no longer

                                , where are you
, elder of sleep & small mercies,
                little conveniences

*

       thoughtful bard in the bone
     & a progress, dreaming itself
                    well into

; if a word does mean,

          river drivers at Martintown,
& shantymen; through the number that drank
       w/ enthusiasm, still

                did make men
     & make

the next winter's ice; breaking ground
logs & the trees,
              listing branches
     in south woods only

       , a premium

*

the marked part less a wound, a
      dream of still waters; a vision or small
, indoctrination; shadows, passing cars
the birds
       & children
                  seeking land
          ; a tablespoon of doubt
to tiny lake, the rhythmic aspect
             of everything
     & the leaves, the lakeshore; last
         unshaven man

       on Saturday night, comes out
           on Sunday morning

slowly approaching himself; if only
         for a moment

*

if accomplishment has nothing to do w/ numbers
        & a myth
                                     a lie
      we can all get behind; easy to mistake
          a deer for deer, or farmer's dog
; a dividend; slip cows & cow bells
& the church bell ringing a connection

          skin & shape of things; imagine
a garden of green & gold-form skirts

dangerous between trees; a sex poem
          deeply uninformed; something

          abt the Bacchae,
      the radical mind

*

a chorus of bluebells, lilies, wild
                by the bridge
                                just south of Greenfield
cattails, a fresh orange grove

                        you just keep growing up
                            & growing

        down the dirty slush
                    of abandoned buildings
            , as water rises

                                    an ambassador in twine

nothing exists
                beyond the darkening side of trees
                beyond the county line

                                amid the stubble
                    of green grass, inheritance
                        of long winter

                                    , nothing

*

the moon rise further; Loyalist moon,
       steady, unchanging, predictable; rediscovering
new words for the names of jars
              & constellations; heavy,

     breath first of ageing, ripe
     daily & the day before

             to exit
the junkyard alive; live & to love
          through tears

       worn patch in jeans; each day
its own expressions, fears
& push of seasons; on,

           unending

   ; moon full of light; my head full of blood

*

the house is not so visible

                                   but from the passing train
                    passenger Ottawa to Montreal
                         for twenty long seconds
                                   , glimpse

                         what occurs; bites little teeth
& fingers;
to be left alone; routine & wandering

        wide, & widening

                         , self-portrait
                         that still has your eyes
.

*

want when I speak your language, want
        & subside; & want again
              , knowing love & necessity
                    not incoherent same

    , in song

            , hello, in a desperate way
writing Moose Creek & Monkland as tires
highway

      sounds full of territory
      & rear view

        if you would fall
        , possibility

of a penny's worth

*

from fenceline open face; Glengarry Scots,
                    an eighteenth-century appeal, the words
can't fail; Loyalist leanings, from New
                        York State, immediately following

the American War of Independence; swallowing words
& miles,
left recent land, from Mohawk Valley north,
                        crossing shores & river boundary

where else would you swim, a hair
                in teeth; impatient
        leaning crash; ruffle features
                    of thick Celtic skin,

maple & oak, cedar boughs, the sky breaks
writing wide, field opens
                                tear stumps
                though limbs a ghost,
                        ghost shadows

        & whisper, although
                        absolutely silent

*

It is a tale full of its endings.
There are all these poems standing
like plumbers amid the ruined buildings
gesturing tool boxes
at the absence of bathrooms in the air, is this
some sort of joke?
And only the Long Sault is laughing:
Fuck your renaissance, get me a beer.
        Don McKay, *Long Sault*

whiskey jack

whiskey jack: A bird (*Perisoreus canadensis*) of North American conifer forests, having grey plumage and a black-capped head. Also called grey jay, camp robber, Canada jay and moosebird. English alteration of *whiskey-john,* from the Cree name "wiss-ka-tjon" or "wis-ka-chon."

Dear Sir: I should like to make sure that everything that I said
    about you in my poetry was true, that you really existed,
That everything that I said was true
That you were not an occasion
In a real bad scene
That what the poems said had meaning
Apart from what the poems said.
        Jack Spicer, *The Collected Books*

I forget: why are there broken birds
behind me: words, goddammit, words.
        John Thompson, *Stilt Jack*

*

beware the conifers, the Grey Jay
in cool northern fall of forests
                    , Lake Superior
or Algonquin Park
                        Tom Thomson
in his sad canoe turns, startled

along the red-cut bank; body
a green tongue
                of forest
& axe; red lumberjack sweater
compares knowledge, purses lips

from bright streaming images, a tree lot
of fresh paint & light, falling
                    leaves, a sunlit
strangeness, empty cloud

burnt rubber & black

doesn't seem to be burning; turns,
looks homeward

*

larger mode, a slice
                              of giving, in
head north, chew thoughtfully
asking, what's in a name?
                              a body of paint
floating Lake Superior knowledge,
& grey bird, somewhat larger
than a robin
                              draw smoke, deep
his powerful, ink-stained lungs
the bird-song lets out, listens
        sudden noises, answers, a reprieve

bare bone nestled
under rock

                stuck on thin, underdeveloped branch,
covered thick by curly hair

am darkly open,
                        ruined

*

what do I encompass, quiet
                    conspiratorial talk, this body
of open wilderness, painted trees
& history that functions
                              without mark
        save seasons

                    three-storey shack, cropped
a tall clay bank at western ledge,
what the birds know
                              animals
& beaver trails on footpath, the
darker wood

        two days shrink an axiom
red summer flecks of hush,
a third-grade switchman
                              eyes like saucers,
windmills, moon

now touched with strange restraint

*

        if you were to touch me, where
would we land; a swift flicker straight
                        across the mouth
& every splinter of thought

                air filled
w/ the air of mountains, a languages of lyre
& living; weird combination of fixity
                    , change

           dollar bills in bird's nest
& three-coloured
        bits of string

                a light that sharpens light

suspended body plops down into pool

*

a fictional zeal was heavied, timeless
                suspension land & hedge,
        the wind rocks trees
                        like moving pictures
of distant disbelief

               beyond the depth of slander,
          boils, violent death but clean,
sentinel platoon of steaming images

        dusk, or dawn

             a ghost-white leaving

*

                         nest in snow
while deep in the ground,
                              for almost a year

the commonness of all things in earth
refuses to migrate, rustling
                  in the hostile winter

                       the wonder of resignation

        the dark stood over watchfully   all through the afternoon

                unafraid, the water
                              & the waters edge

a quiet likely

                        or gliding in flight
            as might float a leaf

*

to remark: a study of birds,
                          two nests
          & a track of movements

                    whisker
                              & blue cowl

hoarding stores upon
                              through ancient snows,
the ones that last till spring
, forever

                    an organ music grinds
                              behind the elbow
                    of two trees

                                        , white-headed children

avalanche

You know this climate like the shape of your hand inside your mitt;
increasing numbness (face licked with cold, ice-slick
questions on your tongue, answers
fewer than you have fingers to count on), familiarity

an avalanche
waiting ...
      Sylvia Legris, *Nerve Squall*

Surely you remember the legendary earthquake.
      Joshua Marie Wilkinson, *lug your careless body out of the careful dusk*

It is simplicity at last.
But what a complicated way of getting happy again.
      George Bowering, "Old Standards"

one

*

avalanche   ;   as in *landslide*
not meaning exactly a disaster but a natural force
a *force of nature*   bombshell blonde

worries, explodes   rips & tears apart
the chain-link fence   do you know
by *not* the name   precision vent & vendor

is rapt or rapture   scallion, eaglet
shorn branches from the wing

                    the mountain face

slides off like shedding skin   ;   I am faithless
& betrayed
                the sun will rise again

        the very taste of iron you

*

is Minotaur, *labyrinthine*
a nest of misses, marks & myths   of *sage*
advice
                 cold capsulated song

middle digit blooms & stutters
a flesh most *capable*   body
in song is most body
                              if where you were leaving
knew anything abt the *price*
(how do you sleep)
                    is fallen bluebeard,
garden-switched, at the beginning (you say)

          of all those *perfectly good men* …

*

am sweeter, sweet   ;   combining love
in a lusty lyric
          ; *my seventh song is breaking*
(& I was thinking)   dawn
           a deal w/ light
, a deliberate strike
          am myriad, akin
volcanic rock & shale
         , a car alarm chirps, the think
            of your sex

     it is next to my flesh

*

the moon makes clouds at last

directed westward, *the wind*   blown up
        from traversable valley

beggars climb, & can't choose   the north
face slides like oil on glass
            shimmeys once & slips

                                        disinterested trees
of possible devastation   ;   how else
                                    to rebuild?

how else to hold a thumb to sky
& wonder *what*?

*

to be an angel + hair   ;   it is
      a different thing to sit behind the sound
, a roar of thunder   ; here I am,
though there you were the rain
               breaking soil & bonds
would you gravity let   ;   let me
           watch you sleeping
      rain can't *keep*
      from falling

*

physics   :   a cumulative process in which
                                  a fast-moving ion or electron generates
                                  further ions & electrons in collision

        suspending   ;   a line from which a line
                                             & so many others
                                                                grow

a belief in air
& you

*

move a subsequent dream   ;   poetical
& street serene
                                        I am wonder
out loud   ;   ground your feet there beneath

I am hastily, silent

                              processional, starved
& seeing stars   ;   fools & ethics, wonder

would you burn from a bridge   ;   or lapse

        the water stone cleft down to bone

every language is a barrier

*

the weight of geography *weighs*
to watch you *sleep*
                                again & again
the car is soluble   ;   water
                                                permission-logged
the way things fall; a pregnant pause mis
carried
                        again, the skin
of sudden vessel
                                        would undergo a rapid
increase in conductivity
            ; where would I take   my
                        many-splendoured

*

if I am remarking tedium   recording
the falling rock
                    smashing bone & bare branch

; hardening
            or octaves, how to build

if I am more ash than complex pressure
or stamen
            carlost   ;   a string field
pulled marionette length of stage

                    a coral sight bleed

I am raw heart at once on the page

                    if I am wearing my hurt
            (today)
                    like a badge

*

the palm of wooded hand   ;   the properties
of sun, moon, air
                        second scent
or spread   ;   *would take*
                            as manual

but would you avalanche you would

        ;   a fruit-fly stand in doorway
        under tables, desk + chair

                        protecting face

*

where is then & art   ;   a magnificent
                                              outpour

malignant grief   strength is stronger
pre-hensile;
           study of cable wire & the car

where your body   would erode
                    me
       moon-mark, article of then-descent

we are Marco, Polo, Marco   stand
           ing *there* in the *water*

waist-deep, wading
           a secular art

*

dear Roy Kiyooka,

                    I know all abt endings
& the terminally begun   ;   have stood
on that back porch, Keefer Street   ;   where once
           your pear tree grew
                     ; each unit
a lyric, grown outward   *you can't step into*
the same river, they say
    but still soaked down to sock & shoe
;   have unconditionally
             loved & broken, blown   ; have
learned
as much forgot
    ;   creating from a simple line
       a mystery
& loving all else

*

is guts & glory   ; hardly
score a snow mass
       come down, descending, go down, fall
hardened
       , the rock face   lifts
(is not afraid)
& separates   ; do you remember yesterday, you said

       the sum an avalanche the rain

; is Everest, worn *a quick picture*
window swells
       my hands went up & fell again

would break out then the *unmeaning* of you

*

according to these calculations
if the colour of rain I deliberately spell
w/ a "u"
                    is shape as well
a landmass of gardens, dulcimer
& mingled measure
                            would *overcome*
artifact of cool spheres
lemon standard of your eyes   ; dangerous
                                         & still

        another hour would   ;
                                    slide

*

a complicated reel
                              ; large lean of falling
&/or sliding material
           ; *arrange my days at elbows*
event that happens, long wind
to a love
                              like a pie left to cool
a breeze persists
over Lake of Two Mountains

                    am standing between doors
; you would yellow leaves your hands

           a sudden appearance of an overwhelming number
           of things

*

if break in the gait;   move downward
& lower
                    not necessarily all the way
a horoscope of generous
trees   ;   that left, my hand
                         your raised pink blouse
; would send & scatter, ginger root

          the whole of avalanche, restraint

the true show of power, & power
in spades   ; if
                         or would
          let loose, instill
a crash or hammer fall

to shake the rumble free, in
still a storm of gravity

                    or thin as a whisper

*

the moon is a crater & fills
    ; my empty spaces
               of snow in the mountains
the plums on the windowsill
are only pears
                      a sudden radiance
of natural event, a happening descent

     engulf, or carry off

           what would we crawl

*

the main break in definition   ;   being *overwhelmed*
not *under*
                    stitch arrival of somesuch
in overwhelming quantity
                              ; stand a field
of avalanche query, slip theory
                                        the roll
& rubble dawn, material slide
a slope of empty
                    single kiss
& how the rest of you
tastes
              to dress & undress, repetition of states
        or to end on an open question

*

to become one   ;   a hardened break
, I would haul your body out
         (what were they saying)
                 , my Orpheus
would never turn or doubt   ;   functional
a song made up of two, three phrases
            ; composed soil, rock
no time but the next time
(I didn't want to leave)
               ; the phone you save my
               twenty messages repeat

      ; the world as an empire
      built of big plate sky

*

a poem of *beginnings*   ;   at the top
                                                    of incremental ski
down devils hill
                    (I am breaking contingencies)
            ; the barometer fell
                        , into each life rain
a body rife w/ collisions & a cellphone false
electronic bells
                        an avalanche of what, snow
            marries hard at the highest point
, sudden shower   think you
in my standing stall
                        a testament
                    to all the weather we lived

*

this indeterminate state of small psalms
& inevitable ends
                              made fragile
        as if not spoken to
                                      ; this mess of correspondence
spread out a tidal wave, start
w/ a single line
              by what you would
              be afraid
; am late in the day & so
electric checkmark
          as a kinder gesture drawn, still knows

*

from the pit of the stomach, a same song
; hardened across bare bone
                                        all acts
are political   ;   or if sleep in the summer,
wintermitts are wind in trees, love
        half beaten Somerset mark
the break in the day you would widen
                                ; a house in the sun
or the dark of the lane where the basketball hoops
        dream the ground out from under

    you   :   would be fingers & toes
                        & can guess how it goes

*

the morning sun tears out   ;   a travesty of light
                                   & light bearings
in a year of ten thousand shades
                how to number   when the Chinese
                   or Hebrew so different
arms will spread out   a dragon drums
                                   Nanny Goat Hill
        ; how can we know?
                                   when the Greeks still hold Christmas
a full two weeks later
        ;   Victoria Day weekend

                                   I wait to overcome
                                   & to *be*

*

dear unnameable,

I have run out of things to tell you
; all possible cloud   *etcetera*
     the rock that all foundations
envy   ; slow on the long road
is a passage of heart   ; *if I*
     had a diary, I would write out your name
avalanche   :   a fundamentally stretched
     become misshapen particle
     ; it is easy to mistake one for another
all boundaries & silence

     what a wonderful display
     (I imagine you radiant,
     knowing full well you are)

or conjoining a calm explosion, finally

two

*

a sweet risotto   ;   even speechless
            I am never done
a force of nature   force
                        of gravity
so strong that even light turns toward to you
dismembered points
                        turning everything invisible
food for thought   ;   me ravenous

*

a characteristic of new cloud   ;   the runout zone
of seasonal   open field
          & relapse of remote places
a dandelion field, some dive in New York
                what is the length   of us
adrift & incomplete   ;   & writing
                                        after
                                                  & all

not in my wildest wings are you waiting; catch
                    as catch can

*

where the hazard lies   ;   frequently created
                    & frequently triggered
          ; the top of a hair's breadth
                    or consequence of machine noise
what else are you?   limitless
, all heartache iron wrought & turn
                    would drive me empty

right me ragged, endless
roughshod off the road

          , sliding rapid down a step

*

I would give it all   ;   once you start,
                          committed
(it doesn't always work)
                                        prone
to mother tongue or lies half-hidden
presumptions based on fact
                    ;   hard-marked essays, hand
          wants more
                                        your arms computer screen
through stretch a side, a full-length blonde
          ; prolonged, a cooling trend in avalanche path
rock & snow & stone throw deep a thousand feet

*

invecting   ;   a real worry
of consequence
                           unacceptable loss of lives
& property
                                 ; *the price of milk*
        if I could anything else   to bear
            every angel wakes neutral
; how to be allowed
                               to pass gravel
              lightly
              & grey highway
& just what falls, or may

                    what else
        is human hope
               but momentarily borne

*

concave, convex or stepped
                              a step down, slow
a mark of long love
        who can't admit slope or shape

an absence

*

to hold my heart a measure
                of (avalanche) activity
in a particular path   ;   if pressure
                                          & support
argue semantic into same
                          ;   two hands
        that hold, or push
                 a beautiful thinking woman
;   of record events   failed evidence
        on straight slopes then on windward slips
                  because the shovelling wind
        on grass slopes then on brush-covered
                akin a lower roughness

this lack of vegetation dive to snowy deep

*

a road or bridge-work structure
   ;   *goes to plant*   a transport blocked
by loving symptoms
     ;   *result, but not the cause*
of one step rubber stamp the days
   of limestone parts & page

        ; stringbound
a signature
     of our naked affections

; if every language lost to this sorry place

*

the end of wonder   ;   it doesn't balance
who would constantly be in place
                              the king
      of the mountain
         ; your blue white breath
         accumulation into air
snow, mud, rock or detached tree
             a breath to throw your
                   arms around
mounds of blocks   ;   a change in depth
                        & cover

      an airtight ravenous kiss

*

another restless day   ;   a noon
        of mistook depth
a downslope mark & down
    , design   of empty names
       & stretched neglect
a sunrise   tipped
       or tipped in
bound & gagged disaster rolls
indistinguishable from one another

*

a geology of taste   ;   an office open door
if every man is waiting
          ;   aggravated by shouts, machine noise, sonic boom

imperil skiers   ;   downhill, cross-country
               would characterize a stanza

genders a pier w/ subsequent rings
                         , rapid-fire floats round

                              there is eventually a silence
                              there is history

          ;   a rocky absolute is less than certain

               is scribbled out between blue spruce

*

how many years
could we have waited   ;   total
              , a hanging cloud, a crack on
                          mountain score

a score of cloud
              well-meaning,
a rudderless boat, delirious, rain
an inevitable catch of books
                                    where
              would you often (regress)

I stepped into
              an avalanche

when life & love go into adolescence

                          in a love between thirty
                          & forty-five degrees

*

acerbate   ;   soft pages
crate a blue air, lilies rose
              if I am reason for you now
a continuous passion
                              of sticks
          & displaced design;   onomatopoeia
causes rift & rigour
                    ; short paste of light
from behind two lines a *movement*

              I am a stain of landscape
I would let you empty
                    & refill

*

a constant array of standing crews
a constant array of springs & falls,
      a rise & a retreat   ;   *run back*

impact/suffocation   ;   the cold air
           breathed in to fleshy lung
     , breed collapse
                 internal
             weather system
                       ; an increase
in the human toll
           ; *am feature clear*

      & am so quick to disappear

*

I just want   ;   in famine
                                                          & haiku
        an ancient root divides
                    (some forgotten aspect of time)
a summer limb   ;   phone call
                                        forgets itself (a rhetoric)
of white legs & limbs

                    would start, return

                    heart w/ the midden in my mouth

*

in twenty seconds grassy warm
      ; *all incomplete* would be *selective*
       (who knew)

a show of hands, a hunger
             in the passionate air

   (in other words)

   what drives would do, attend so well?

*

dear endless

          what would tenor be
sung mute?   a list of lips
& worry no longer
            ; women I would
            no longer need
            to forget
; this hopeful mire
        to know
    one only

                would you

& once again I dropped, I fell

*

when we are not but *almost*
     ; an entire day to concentrate

a shared shouldered entry
                    (what is my tone?)
             a mouth of stars & sum
                         a travelling source as wet
                         your hair
Ottawa line a path explaining space
;   what space there is

            a series of entries, broken

                  (the red shape of miracles)

*

a basic stitch of leaves   ;   iron ore
      & flakes the stream bring gold & silver vein
entirely the moment
                 a dynamic female
elegant to complex pressures
        ; *wood bred down to diamond, coal*
learning observation stark
             by heart
    is this what hollows
; an attention of the pressured space
            , canary's burnished lungs

    crossing centuries adequate to embrace

    selective line of snow beneath
         (a memory)

*

mistake distrust
      ; don't take w/ alcohol, while driving
      or doing anything else that requires
                          concentration
the Advil logical flaw   ;   one
                                     & one
                                   , one
at thirty-six years would sing unbid
                , the grinning weeping love or of
to improve my game
                        the new rain
      comes again at last

        I would listen you slow to sea

*

what an active eye can do   ;   turn in
         to rate an angle
      ; *conditions of the soil*   rate mulch
                                              & stage
infer rain buckles   ; sleep me
                                             , *windswept*

       (how *do* you sleep)

a corner of firm & a grey state

         I am fact & hands only; mouth; arms
                 & open legs

*

the more I melt

                         the more I listen

     ; chicken & egg

          what do you do w/ silence?

*

but what is an aesthetic
of wonderful destruction, an avalanche splintered
   unquiet down   ; deep
             as a kiss
or a seventh wave ; a hazard until man
, roar crashing clean white swath through grime
     ; dust-covered row
upon row   ; deeper, denser
    help mark outer rim

   I would windlessly erase

once it begins, what kind of frequency
of such   traditions of meaning, edge
   such clear extensive damage

       to speak itself enough through speaking

*

dear avalanche

       to even wonder ;   to even
                            unmake more
is to keep (me) from being destroyed
                                what
does a heart make   ;   a house
w/ endless windows
                        oh what ears
we waste on other nonsense, warnings
& fears
          the not gained, given
                      a tip in
wonders, does *wonders*
;   *would embrace each other in darkness*

          oh slip of gravity & mass

              ; *come darken*

three

*

dear selected ruin

                  the sight of you *leaving*

; as mouth the

      mouth of you

                I have never been so

                glad to be

                        / *broken*

a sunset of balconies

                ; ruined

      no longer

      the names of all my broken hearts

      are only names again

*

if it be your will   ;   an avalanche
                                    location safe
                    if I am future, you
                        ;   alternatives might
how the chances of survival
                                    ; a burning building,
                                    love
                as vests & airbags
                            ; *any group*
                        must be capable of self-rescue

I would walk you thin
            , unmoved   ;   the strength
                                        I know

                    (that) you have in

*

during the course of temperature   ;
                    precipitation & wind
; medium latitudes
                         arm in an arm
the way your body leans
                              soft caress
         oh, soft & supple medium

a tree would you
              remember (me)

would you feel the blossom worn thin
falling
         the bud   a sprung line
                 free of complication?

*

after a visual search   ;   of surface
                                                   clues
          a through-location, digging snow
(where are you, heart?)
                             a hand
                    through fisted wall (in tow)
;   a large scoop, sturdy handle
                         (in way of things)

                 important   ;   a reliance on birds
                                    to summon

a discount blend of facts
                    ; both real,

                    imagined

*

an instability   ;   an overlying slab
        ; observable properties of snow

through thin silver dust of moon

                ; where, on long-lost snow
                & dream of the snow

                        dream of you dear heart
                                , drifting, in

slow
        & stumble   ;
                                never drifting

*

dear hurricane

        you have nothing on me
this poem refers to a natural event

    ; a sheltered mess
of rock, large snow

          a piecemeal act
      , recovery
         , delivered out

; poems only an illusion
against destructive slide

      ; rebuilding
   want

        out of you so much
          more

*

an uninterrupted heart ;   of staggers depth
    if you were any   *in*
          capable speech
words believe you
        ; if   &   *only*

    out loud, pray
              I am desire-sight,
I am night-known
        folly
    for these engineered escapes

      would we *imply* or *impune*

a dusty, salted fact
or critter

*

not a fear of desperation
or of need   ;   or even
                                          want
                    but a simple understanding
;   a series of soft, inevitable

the avalanche will come   a lowered heart

                    I am wrought w/ this
                    I have flavoured meaning words
                              & so much this
                                        , incoming

          through body what; is insurmountable

*

dear long distance

        when I am sufficiently spent, away
a Bathurst phone booth not the space
   to house this oversized heart   ;   the point
                    last seen

   ; night terrors spent

       would also

weather hazards   ;   *known* not *lower angled*

   ; the stops enlarge the air
   & mark ice further fate
            , sealed

     (is)

*

to fold her garden   *slow*
       ly   ;   meaning *you*

the delicate erase & ease of *comes*
              out swinging   heart
      schemata
        , lost for good
            or would you
gleaming, out
       or virginal
          mad w/ grief

    renewed, at times

        a starfish coin

       if substance could not but sing

*

from Wikipedia, the free encyclopedia:

> "if you find yourself in a potentially dangerous
> avalanche situation, you should seriously question
> the choice of route, why your safety is being put
> in jeopardy, and what alternatives might be safer
> than pressing on."

*

dear Frank Slide

            for all that you held, nether stone
one hundred later years   ;   bodies buried by rock
                         & remain
the worst natural disaster
                  in then-country
the town of Frank buried
      & its offspring, Frank Slide
            a mile more down road
                     , continued

leaning out a storm or story

*

if I am seismic, you
                    ;   inefficient ends
        a careful glow
                of *marked as searched*
;   what runoff of debris, the bottom low
                        & edges track
"couldn't find you anywhere,
                    and was looking
                            very hard."
        if we could call on fruitful scare,
                    charcoal winters
bask of trees & undone sun

            ; how many years were we unknown
                            not found?
        ; how many years can bodies bloom & spend
                    & break to rebuild?

*

a spring fling summer

I feel seismic, magnetically attracted

if I could write a book of words like small birds
        , meaningful
                    , full of flight

*

if I am sudden
      interrupted, is not
quickly so   ;   *a nest of it*
or would have taken

                      a moment to open,
                      a crack
& spread wide   (as you know)
                  ; a calculus of warm gear
                  delays hypothermia
                            (if buried)

      near zero after hour two

      the chances of survival

                  as in winter

*

consequently it is *vital*   ;   an immediate
                                       search & rescue
          ; operated out of *everyone*
girl & Supergirl
                    , the rail suspends the core
of eccentricities, meticulous & limitless
                                   ; a tone to the heart
          or tunnel
                         would engineer
                         a pre-determined length
; is radical
                    a long-term depth,
                                   idea

          the only one worth having

*

if my own skin eats time
partial   or complete   ; figures
          in burnt sun, scope
of *what else, other*   *I become we*
; one becomes abstract

                    & fragment   ; less known
                              knowable
          as would expand & not contain our growth

; am theory spent

               , a thing is not a thing until

*

sex at thirty-six

                what do I remember
from those heady bygones
        (have I even met you yet);   a hill or fare-thee-well
; *gone fishin'*
         ;   *elevator*
where is your talent for decoding
or descending
          ; a river run, avalanche
       to emerge from a glacier
                 warm, & unchanged
an elongated drift,
            supply of casual
            & causal flow

       am suspended & sorry-worn
;   not a telephone alive gets answered

afterword: The green-wood essay: a little autobiographical dictionary

When Crusoe landed on his island after the shipwreck, he was not yet Robinson. He would be Robinson from the moment that, finding neither pen nor pencil in the jetsam, he liberated a cutter and some books. From these found objects would be born the method that names him.

> Emmanuel Hocquard, "Robinson Method,"
> ed./trans. Norma Cole, *Crosscut Universe:*
> *Writing on Writing from France*

The real knowledge of weather is indigenous.

> Lisa Robertson, "The Weather:
> A Report on Sincerity," *Chicago Review*

1.

I sometimes talk about my home, my point of origin, as though it isn't there anymore. Less than an hour's drive from where I'm sitting. The red-bricked house still stands, my father lives where he has always lived. Now widower, less a year. On summer Saturdays, he possibly still claims riding mower from the shed to cut surrounding lawn, up both sides of the lane. Can you ever go home again? Why would you wish to? I don't want to regress to some sentimental or imagined security from my nineteenth year, the summer I finally left; I want to be as I am, visiting that place I used to live, despite knowing that imaginary photo-still less intact with every visit. Leonard Cohen's quote about returning regularly to his hometown, Montreal, to "renew his neurotic afflictions." One has to reconcile differences, and the results of time's inevitable passage. My father eases into the end of his seventh decade and the barn now abandoned more than a dozen years. He uses it as storage, the former milkhouse now a woodworking shop. The barnyard barren, overgrown. Whether I am home or not, an anchor. To live at all, one must get used to loss. One must acknowledge gains.

I compare the current state of barn to a corpse, a dead thing. What was once a living, thriving creature. Empty of livestock, feral cats, component parts of milking equipment salvaged, sold. What's left of the structure slowly rotting, more than a century old. The hewn beams in the haymow suggest it rebuilt from a previous structure, one we never knew.

My former partner in Toronto didn't fully comprehend the weight, the security such connections bring; I'm not sure my late mother did, either, with childhood residences listing years in Brockville, Kemptville, Ottawa. My father, the same house since a year old, born across the dirt road in the little house my sister shares with husband, three kids; a log house said to be older than Dominion. The farm next door, where my grandfather, great-grandfather born as well, home as well to two generations further, going back on this stretch of Macdonald's Grove to 1845. This, I know, remains.

2.

Ralph Connor, pen name of the Rev. Charles Gordon, considered Canada's best-selling author at the turn of the century. Highly moral novels about the Glengarry Scots of the upper Ottawa Valley, when Gaelic probably still first language. Generations of McLennans raised in the church his father built, late eighteenth-century red steeple held the morals of a community, dour Protestantism, with that silent, Calvinist streak. As Connor himself wrote in *Postscript to Adventure, The Autobiography of Ralph Connor* (1938): "Our Glengarry folk, as I have said, were mostly from the Highlands and Islands of Scotland. They were sturdy, industrious, patient, courageous." How important his books were as an example to me, to realize it was possible to be from here, and write. Perhaps not temporally local but geographically, to realize there was such a thing as serious art amid this wooded glen where history preferred. The little one-room schoolhouse now at Upper Canada Village, where paternal grandmother studied, some four decades after Connor. Only later, my late teens into my early twenties, aware of the work of Dorothy Dumbrille, Don McKay. Gary Geddes, Henry Beissel, Stephen Brockwell. Glengarry books, and even authors.

3.

Through the space of my lifetime, the Canadian population
has gone from being predominantly rural to predominantly
urban. Russell Smith's deliberately urban novels, exploring a
real space currently lived. I grew up on a dairy farm, five miles
from a village. At the University of Alberta, an MA student who
didn't realize that writers also originated from farms thought
Canadian rural was an arbitrary literary construct. You have got
to be kidding me. There are those of us still from farm country
composing literary books, our individual poems. Karen Solie,
Robert Kroetsch, Phil Hall, Sheri Benning, Dennis Cooley. The
poets from small towns: Andy Weaver, Adam Dickinson, Don
McKay, Monty Reid. I came from a long line of farmers. Is it
really so rare? How many literary writers of my generation can say
the same? How can that not impact upon my relationship with
space itself, a relationship with the land? So different from the
suburban spaces of Sheila Heti, Michael Holmes, Anne Stone,
David McGimpsey or Jon Paul Fiorentino. Barbara Gowdy.

4.

Pastoral. Don McKay talks about it, Lisa Robertson references
it. More than just the weather. There have even been a few
anthologies. What has this to do with writing? Not arbitrary
and artificially writing about the natural world, but simply being
aware of spaces. Listen.

What happens outside can't help but impact upon our immediate.
The corn won't be ready for another few days. If it rains, we can't
cut the hay today. Wait for the sun to dry bales in the field. If wet
bales of hay or straw in the haymow, trapped and pressurized,
wet heat begins to boil, burst into flame. This is how you lose the
barn, the herd. How you can smell the rain in the air for miles,
anticipate it through the way the wind blows through the leaves.
A sudden drop in temperature, and pressure. My father, who
knows the names of trees, the birds, the long wild grasses. Less
deliberate than birding. More.

How we talk about the weather. How these systems directly
impact the way a growing season unfolds, and subsequent year.
All the way to the bank. Just how much you need to understand

the earth, the weather, the way the wind blows, to be able
to make any kind of living. It is a question of survival. The
immediate becomes a seasonal cycle, more important than school,
than birthdays, anniversaries. We mark our days by cycles of
planting, harvest. Spring, when the soil is dry enough to till, a
whole new crop of stones to pick, and overflow front-end loader,
decorate fence line. To harvest these before a proper till, before
the rows of seed. Not stone hammer or stone maul but simple
stone, scraped up by scar of plow.

5.

Instead of recess, played my scales. Another lesson. A further
removal from bonding with peers, already quiet, shy. Out on the
farm, with barely a neighbour my age. Thirteen years of lessons,
told to practise instead of wasting, wandering time. I wasted time.
I put my head down. Played. I suppose, then, this was discipline.
Certain notions set aside.

I absorbed books, consumed them. Wrote poems, small stories,
painted pictures, drew, took photographs. Self-taught guitar.
Studied the shadows of clouds as they eased their slow way across
hayfields, after the second summer cut. The dust cloud of mail
delivery down dirt road. Walk up the lane to harvest weekday mail
and daily paper, dog running excited circles. The days that once the
mail, often little else external interfered. Much the way I still live.

Solitary exploration, a matter of course. So many times, the dog
in tow. Exploring the trails through the bush beside what now my
sister's house, once where my grandmother widowed, some fifteen
years alone. The trail that opened up a mouth and mossy mound
rose feet away the rotting decades of my grandfather's maple sugar
shack. To the left, much farther down, the sandpit where we once
dumped our early 1970s garbage. The sand, the garbage, long
removed, the trail grown over. Other threads and other paths
since opened, wide enough to roll a tractor; dual ruts, hauling
once-wood for the basement furnace. The unknown corners
where he set late family pets to rest, unrecorded cats and dogs.
Not met with oblivion but return; they are there, still.

The world outside the house a language that requires itself
to be understood, if one is to depend on such for livelihood,

direction. Inside the farmhouse, another sort of language existed, constructed out of singular, similar silences. Codes not taught or explained, and often defying comprehension. Learning another language by rote, by trial and error. We would not speak, thus.

6.

Poet Phil Hall speaks of tokens, essential remnants, markers. The heart of history engages and emerges from our objects, often. A washboard from cobwebbed basement, my grandfather's ancient film camera, his shaving travel case I carry. Who we are and where we're from a thing constantly renegotiated, something carried within, no matter where we might end up. Foundations rarely change, no matter subsequent constructions.

My apartment is littered. Tokens, large and small. Hall's fill up the barn behind his Perth-area cottage. What do these magpie tendencies, these impulses, mean? Where do they take us? Or do they stabilize. Not hold back, nor hold in place.

7.

Is it possible to be pastoral in a city? Does a city provide, not an automatic relationship with the land but with ideas? When you pave the bare earth over, does your relationship become distant, distracted, even artificial? Not so, I know. Still. Hot sun bounces off concrete back up, resonates further heat. Is not absorbed into the still-cool earth. In a big city, under a tree in the shadiest part of cool, of park.

The predominant work of my twenties, learning to read the language of cities. The rumble of OC Transpo bus around the corner, felt before seen. Navigating sidesteps from the breath of exhaust, a patch of water splashed from passing cars. Identify the direction of smoke before the strawberry lights and wail of sirens locate. The reduced ice build-up on the north sidewalks of Centretown east-west streets that winter sun provides, the shade of cooler south for summer. The patterns of traffic lights.

Attention, even before any conversation concerning wilderness as subject. A city pastoral, the wilderness that lives in collaboration with our attempts, insistences, on domesticity. Control. Is still a wild animal. Trees live no differently than in the wild, and birds as well, adapting. When these adaptations take, wouldn't our pastorals shift as well? A matter of attention, beyond eco-poetry, beyond green. Already there, part of a system larger than ourselves, one we should simply admit to being part of.

Seasons shift, the rain. The shifts in weather that tear down fragile barriers, monuments to our imagined, shallow attempts at dominance. No matter how we try. New Orleans.

The rain still streams down Nanny Goat Hill, rolling west down Somerset West to Preston Street. The world exists, and here we are, a part.

8.

What this, pastoral. So called. So often dismissed for how deeply it is misconstrued, needlessly reduced. Ignoring the boundaries for the oversimplifications. Why border such at all? Why forsake the wilderness entirely for only fields? Not merely metaphor-driven lyric narratives, but a matter of attention. Not as Anne Simpson alludes in her *The Marram Grass: Poetry & Otherness* (2009), a poetry, a pastoral, separate from the natural world, but a human consideration and experience already a component part; exploring relationships I would argue, instead, between the two. We already live in the world, why pretend to be apart? Include Monty Reid's *Flat Side* (1998), Barry McKinnon's *Pulp/Log* (1991), or Don McKay's *Long Sault* (1975). Margaret Christakos' *Not Egypt* (1989), *Welling* (2010). Karen Solie's *Pigeon* (2009). Phil Hall's *The Little Seamstress* (2010). Ken Belford. Peter Culley. For example.

This is about attention, not of stepping back into how poems once were, should be. This is an attempt to pay attention. Pay attention.

Acknowledgments

> This book is for my parents,
> Douglas & Joanne
> my daughter Kate,
> my sister Kathy,
> & her three children,
> Emma, Rory & Duncan

Thanks so much to Sandra Ridley, who made insightful comments on a much-earlier draft. Thanks to the example of Don McKay through his *Long Sault*. Essential thanks to Karl Siegler for ongoing support, encouragement and faith.

glengarry: open field: The piece "glengarry: open field" is my Glengarry County version of Barry McKinnon's *Pulp/Log*, and owes a degree of thanks to that as well as Don McKay's *Long Sault* (which someone [namely Chaudiere] should reprint as a single unit), furthering my side of the conversation that began with my second trade poetry collection, *bury me deep in the green wood* (ECW Press, 1999). Thanks, too, to a number of random source texts I riffed off (in varying degrees): Sina Queyras (ed.) *Open Field: 30 Contemporary Canadian Poets* (Persea Books, 2005), Mark Wallace and Steven Marks (eds.) *Telling it Slant: Avant-Garde Poetics of the 1990s* (University of Alabama Press, 2002), my own *side/lines: a new Canadian poetics* (Insomniac Press, 2002), William Carlos Williams' *Paterson* (New Directions), Royce MacGillivray and Ewan Ross' *A History of Glengarry* (Mika Publishing, 1979), Rebecca Wolff (ed.) *Fence* magazine, volume 8, numbers 1&2 (summer 2005), & of course, never in that order. Plenty of other references hidden within as well.

avalanche: Thanks very much to all the people who read or heard earlier versions of the text and responded, including Lea Graham, Sarah Ruffolo, Nathaniel G. Moore and Gregory Betts. Thanks, too, to The Art Bar Reading Series in Toronto, where I was able to read most of the first two sections, June 6, 2006, and Thomas Wharton, who hosted a reading of the same at the University of Alberta, November 15, 2006. Composed from May 14 to June 13, 2006. Unofficial soundtrack: "Avalanche" by Leonard Cohen and "King of the Mountain" by Kate Bush. The piece was produced in book form by Jessica Smith's Outside Voices as *Outside Voices Take-Home Project #4* in 2006 in an edition of one, and later, by Apostrophe Press, Ottawa, for a reading at The Carleton Tavern, August 28, 2009 (with Nicholas Lea and Stephen Cain) in a numbered edition of twenty copies.